FORERUNNERS: IDEAS FIRST FROM THE UNIVER...
MINNESOTA PRESS

Original e-works to spark ne

FORERUNNERS: IDEAS FIRST i
breakthrough digital works. Wri
ished books, Forerunners draws o ....ated in notable blogs, social media, conference plenaries, journal articles, and
the synergy of academic exchange. This is gray literature publishing: where intense thinking, change, and speculation take place in
scholarship.

Shareveillance

Shareveillance
The Dangers of Openly Sharing
and Covertly Collecting Data

Clare Birchall

University of Minnesota Press

MINNEAPOLIS

Portions of this book were previously published in a different form as "Shareveillance: Between Open and Closed Data," *Big Data and Society* 3, no. 2 (2016), and in "'Data.gov-in-a-Box': Delimiting Transparency," *European Journal of Social Theory* 18, no. 2 (2015): 185–202. Both of these articles were published by SAGE Publications Ltd. All rights reserved. Copyright Clare Birchall.

Published by the University of Minnesota Press, 2017
111 Third Avenue South, Suite 290
Minneapolis, MN 55401-2520
http://www.upress.umn.edu

The University of Minnesota is an equal-opportunity educator and employer.

For Eden

Contents

Preface

WHEN MY DAUGHTER WAS SMALL, and possessions, to her, held talismanic qualities, I would frequently extoll the virtues of sharing. Sharing was something that didn't seem to come naturally to her but had to be learned. In an attempt to sell my daughter on the idea of sharing, I emphasized the benefits in terms of both social capital ("People won't like you if you don't share") and access to a wider range of goods, promising a *kinder*-commons ("If you share with others, they will share with you"). As will become clear, I am not so unequivocal about sharing in the realm of digital data, though many are. Mirroring my parental evangelism regarding sharing, there is a dominant discourse that emphasizes the advantages of digital sharing. This short book builds on almost a decade of research I have conducted into the politics of transparency and secrecy to consider a form of subjectivity and a politics produced by the calls that are made on citizens and states to share and be transparent and render data open. I will argue that it is not simply an irony that such calls are made alongside a continued investment in infrastructures and practices of state secrecy and forms of closed data. Rather, both open and closed data practices produce what I call a shareveillant subject.

Introduction: The Disunited States of Sharing

TWO QUESTIONS DOMINATE current debates at the intersection of privacy, governance, security, and transparency: How much and what kind of data should citizens have to *share* with surveillant states? and How much data from government departments should states *share* with citizens? Yet, these issues are rarely expressed in terms of "sharing" in the way that I do in this book. More often, when thought in tandem with the digital, *sharing* is used in reference to free trials of software (shareware); the practice of peer-to-peer file sharing; platforms that facilitate the pooling, borrowing, swapping, renting, or selling of resources, skills, and assets that have come to be known as the "sharing economy"; or the business of linking and liking on social media, which invites us to share our feelings, preferences, thoughts, interests, photographs, articles, and Web links. Sharing in the digital context has been framed as a form of exchange, then, but also as communication and distribution (see John 2013; Wittel 2011).

To understand the politics of open and opaque government data practices that share with citizens or ask citizens to share, I will extend existing commentaries on the distributive qualities of sharing by drawing on Jacques Rancière's (2004b) notion of the "distribution of the sensible"—a settlement that determines what is visible, audible, sayable, and knowable and what share or role we each have within it. In the process, I articulate "sharing" with "veillance" (*veiller*, "to watch," is from the Latin *vigilare*, from *vigil*, "watchful") to turn the focus from prevalent ways of understanding digital sharing toward a form of contemporary subjectivity. What I call *shareveillance*, a state in which we are always already sharing—indeed, in which any relationship with data is only made possible through a conditional idea of sharing—produces an antipoliticized public made up of shareveillant subjects caught between the affects and demands of different data practices.

Although it is tempting to use the term *depoliticized* here, I use *antipoliticized*, because it better captures the way in which shareveillant practices both invoke political agency and yet severely delimit it, not least by the way in which, for example, they encourage actions framed by the notion of choice and the citizen qua consumer. Moreover, *depoliticized* might imply nostalgia for a once fully agential autonomous subject—and we know from psychoanalysis, post-Marxism, and poststructuralism, among other discourses, that the subject has always been fragmented; shot through with blind spots, absence, and lack; divided and endlessly divisible. I am interested, therefore, in the ways in which shareveillance forecloses politics even while seeming to foster forms of democratic engagement with governance through open data.

This book operates under the assumption that both open and opaque government data initiatives involve, albeit differently pitched, forms of sharing and veillance. Government practices that share data with citizens involve veillance because they call on citizens to monitor and act on that data—we are envisioned (watched and hailed) as auditing and entrepreneurial subjects.

Citizens have to monitor the state's data, that is, or they are expected to innovate with it and make it profitable. Data sharing therefore apportions responsibility without power. It watches citizens watching the state, delimiting the ways in which citizens can engage with that data and, therefore, the scope of the political per se.

Opaque government data practices (practices that we cannot see through, that are not readily knowable), such as those enacted by the National Security Agency (NSA) and the Government Communications Headquarters (GCHQ) via the PRISM, Tempora, and XKeyscore surveillance programs, as revealed by Edward Snowden, produce "closed" data. The main point about closed data in relation to the state (and it is important to note at the outset that the details would be different for commercial enterprises) is that it is withheld from general access and circulation for reasons concerned with diplomacy, stability, power play, or security.[1] Despite the sense of restriction, claim, and withholding here, opaque government data practices still involve sharing, however, not least because they require citizens to (often unknowingly) "share" data with the veillant state in a way that renders them visible and trackable.

But we should not think of the positions carved out for citizens in each configuration as oscillating between agency and impotence. Nor is it quite right to think of this as the "equiveillance" diagnosed by Steve Mann (2013)—an evenly poised balance between surveillant and sousveillant forces. Rather, shareveillance constitutes the antipoliticized role the datafied neoliberal security state imagines for its public; the latter is

1. The United Kingdom's Open Data Institute, which works with public and private entities promoting innovation through open data, defines closed data as "data that can only be accessed by its subject, owner or holder" (Broad 2015).

configured more as either a flat data set or a series of individual auditor-entrepreneurs than as a force with political potential. For those of us unhappy with politics being delimited and disavowed in this way, we will need to experiment with ways to interrupt shareveillant subjectivity that do not in any way play into or endorse the "post-truth" disavowal (or even disappearance) of facts and data under populist figures like Donald Trump.[2]

A radical critique of ubiquitous and default "sharing" in the digital context is clearly necessary, but I also want to seek out opportunities to salvage the concept of "sharing" to imagine a collective political subjectivity that could emerge from within this sociotechnical moment (rather than pitching one against it). In this book, then, I will propose that we can interrupt shareveillant subjectivity by claiming, not a right to access more and more data or a right to privacy, but a "right to opacity" (Glissant 1997).[3] In the context of shareveillance, I am imagining this right as the demand not to be reduced to, and interact with, data in ways delimited by the state—to resist the terms of engagement set by the two faces of shareveillance (i.e., sharing data with the state and monitoring shared data). The formulation of such an argument rests on an appropriation of the term *sharing* by calling on the etymological roots of *to share*—particularly the Old English for portion *(scearu)*, which points toward a cutting, a shearing, a part or division. With this in mind, we can imagine a right to opacity that cuts into and

2. See the afterword.
3. I want to acknowledge at the very beginning that I am aware that this is not an unproblematic borrowing. The roots of this phrase in critical race theory are often erased and underplayed when invoked, as they increasingly are, in other contexts. I would like to thank Zach Blas for introducing me to Glissant's thought some years ago and for questioning its use in different contexts.

apart veillant formations and data distributions through various tactics, such as hacking, data obfuscation, decentralization, encryption, and anarchic algorithms. Accepting shareveillance means accepting a "distribution of the sensible" that is not based on equality, necessitating a different, more ethical distribution, cut, or share by way of a response on our part. Exploring a right to opacity in the face of shareveillance can politicize the concept of "sharing" by envisioning it as an equitable, ethical cut.

1. Sharing Digitally

MUCH EXCITEMENT has accompanied the rise of the "sharing economy" as facilitated by digital technologies, but so too has critique. If the dominant discourse celebrates this economy for its entrepreneurial ability to utilize spare capacity (usually with regard to for-profits like Uber and Airbnb rather than nonprofits like Freecycle), skeptics focus on the neoliberal erosion of labor rights and safeguards and the commercialization of communitarianism. Gary Hall (2016, 17), for example, points out that

> even if this form of economy is presented as a revival of community spirit, it actually has very little to do with sharing access to goods, activities and services, and everything to do with selling this access. . . . It thus does hardly anything to challenge economic inequality and injustice.

What Mike Bulajewski (2014) finds unpalatable is the way in which the utopianism expressed in populist studies like Yochai Benkler's (2006) *The Wealth of Networks* and Clay Shirky's (2008) *Here Comes Everybody,* as well as in rhetoric accompanying the sharing economy more generally, "conflates political action and market transaction."

The use of the term to refer to a range of platforms and apps that facilitate the harnessing of surplus time, skills, goods, and capacities is only the latest incarnation of sharing's articulation within the digital context.[1] Nicholas John (2013) lobbied for "sharing" to be considered as a keyword for understanding digital culture, in the tradition of Raymond Williams (1976). Subsequently, "sharing" is included in *Culture Digitally*'s Digital Keywords.[2] John's (2014) contribution to that project mentions sharing in terms of three examples. First, he calls on computer time sharing, which was developed during the late 1950s and early 1960s to make efficient use of expensive processor time. Second, John includes file sharing, which informed the U.S. Department of Defense's development of ARPAnet and was strengthened by the introduction of Transmission Control Protocol (TCP)/Internet Protocol (IP) in 1973, based on the network guiding packets to their destination. Subsequent protocols, such as Hypertext Transfer Protocol (HTTP) and Simple Mail Transfer Protocol (SMTP), develop the concept that networks can facilitate direct connections and transfers between hosts. Recent peer-to-peer file-sharing techniques present the latest evolution of such logic (see Johnson, McGuire, and Willey 2008, 2). Third, John mentions *data sharing* as the term that has, after Snowden, come to denote the simple transportation of data. Though all three of these make an appearance, John chooses to focus on a fourth instance: one embedded in the logic of Web 2.0. In this discussion, he turns to the way in which social networking sites have appropriated the term *shar-*

1. It is not within the scope of this book to address the extra- or predigital history of "sharing," but, as Russell Belk (2010, 730) puts it, it is "likely the oldest type of consumption."

2. Digital Keywords is a forum hosted by the University of Tulsa, which took inspiration from the fortieth anniversary of Raymond Williams's 1976 *Keywords*. It is available at http://culturedigitally.org /digital-keywords/. The entries have been published in a collection with Princeton University Press (Peters 2016).

ing to refer to the imperative and logic of communication and distribution. Because posting, linking, and liking are all termed "sharing" on social networking sites, John (2013, 176) claims that, in effect, "sharing is the fundamental and constitutive activity of Web 2.0."

This imperative toward sharing, and the implicit interpolation involved, is well satirized by David Eggers (2013) in his dystopian novel *The Circle*. Mae, a new employee and rising star at the eponymous Google-like behemoth, invokes the aphorism "Sharing is Caring" (302). After a number of coercive, disciplinary encounters in which the company's expectations (to "share"; to be transparent; to contribute to the data set) are made explicit, Mae also comes to believe that holding back one's experiences, even those previously classed as "private," from the network is tantamount to theft (303). If one does not share digitally, if one does not acquiesce to the datafied subjectivity imagined by the Circle, one is denying the possibility of commensurability between data and world; the full saturation of digital knowledge banks; a comprehensive big data set enabling predictive health and policing; absolute cognitive mapping for a digital totality—what the CEOs of the Circle refer to, somewhat chillingly, as "completion."

As *The Circle* makes clear, in addition to acting in the service of communication, sharing data also has to be understood as a form of distribution. Human and nonhuman actors are involved in the dissemination of data, documents, photos, Web links, feelings, opinions, and news across space and time. Such an obvious point is worth making because it allows us to think beyond the dominant, morally inflected imperative to share or connect with others in a network through a confessional–communicative style toward circulation in a purely spatial sense (albeit one with ethicopolitical implications). It might be useful here to think about such a process as one of *spatial differentiation*—a term borrowed from economics and that re-fers to the uneven dispersal of resources, goods, and services. Differences in natural and human resources lead to inequitable access to inputs and outputs. I want to retain this inflection—of inequality, disparity—with the intention that it will open the way for a broader discussion of the politics or ethics of (data) veillance, distribution, and sharing, in the context of the state rather than private platforms.

2. Distribution of the (Digital) Sensible

WHEREAS John's (2013, 176) use of the term *distribution* points toward the act of disseminating photos, files, videos, and so on, I'm going to draw on its appearance in the lexicon of Jacques Rancière. Rancière's (2004b) *Le Partage du Sensible* is translated as a sharing, partition, division, and, more commonly, distribution of the sensible. This distribution of the sensible is an aesthetico-political settlement. It is, in Rancière's words,

> a delimitation of spaces and times, of the visible and the invisible, of speech and noise, that simultaneously determines the place and the stakes of politics as a form of experience. Politics revolves around what is seen and what can be said about it, around who has the ability to see and the talent to speak, around the properties of spaces and the possibilities of time. (12–13)

Aesthetics for Rancière is a distributive regime determining what action, reaction, and thought are possible in any given situation. It is political precisely because, in every "distribution of the sensible," equality is either undermined or affirmed as what is common and what is exclusive becomes apparent. A distribution determines "those who have a part in the community of citizens" (7); it "reveals who can have a *share* in what is common to the community based on what they do and on the time and space in which this activity is performed" (8, emphasis added). Equality is enacted or verified when those without part, the unrepresented, come to take part, when those without a share have a share. In a process of subjectivization,[1] this involves refuting the subject position one is allocated by the system and finding a position, as well as a name or identity-in-relation, that will enable full participation and recognition—akin to the work the term *proletariat* once might have performed (Rancière 1992). An instantiation of politics, which for Rancière has to verify a presupposed equality, is when demands for a new division and sharing of the social whole are granted to those rendered invisible and unheard.

Such a conception can be helpful in the context of open and opaque government digital data practices and the shareveillant subjectivity that connects them (which I will come to later). It makes sense today to include digital data in an understanding of the sensible (that which can be seen, heard, touched, thought). Its availability to a subject's veillant capacities or range and the conditions of its visibility (to whom, in which circumstances, to what ends) are usefully thought as part of a particular distribution. In any encounter, we can ask, "Who has a share of the data?" and "What kind of subjectivity is made more likely as a result of that division and/or access?" Before turning to discuss these questions in terms of open and opaque government data practices in more detail, I want to pause on the logic of sharing as it pertains to the digital in general, for through this I hope to demonstrate a technological underpinning to the rise of shareveillance.

1. See Chambers (2012) on the different incarnations of this term— *subjectivation* and *subjectification*.

3. Sharing as Protocological Condition

RETURNING to John's (2013, 176) claim that "sharing is the fundamental and constitutive activity of Web 2.0," it is important to note that later, he pushes this further. "It could even be argued that . . . the entire internet is fundamentally a sharing technology" (179), he writes, citing the importance of open source software and programming languages, and sharing economies of production, in the development of websites based on user-generated content. Likewise, Engin Isin and Evelyn Ruppert (2015, 89) claim that "the ubiquity of various uses of digital traces has made data sharing the norm." While I'm also interested in sharing configured in this way, I want to slightly rephrase and shift the emphasis of these assertions to suggest that sharing can be conceived as the constitutive logic of the Internet. Rather than thinking about sharing primarily as something that users *do* on the Internet, then, I want to focus more on the idea that sharing operates at a protocological level. My use of this term here draws on Alexander Galloway's (2004, 7) exposition of computer protocols as standards that "govern how specific technologies are agreed to, adopted, implemented, and ultimately used by people around the world."

In arguing this point, I want to be clear that I am not supporting a utopian celebration of the Internet's open, or free, origins. Galloway, among others, makes the error of such an assumption clear, as he characterizes the Internet as a technology marked by control and hierarchies of enclosure. Rather, in positing sharing as protocological, I want to imply simply that the Internet's grain is, first and foremost, "stateless" in the sense that programming intends: as a lack of stored inputs. In other words, the basic architecture of the Internet does not automatically keep a record of previous interactions, and so each interaction request is handled based only on the information that accompanies it. For example, the Internet's fundamental method for sending data between computers, IP, works by sending small chunks of data, "packets," that travel independently of each other. These discrete packets are put together at an upper layer, by TCP, yet IP itself operates without state. We can also look to how the Web's HTTP serves up requested pages but does not "remember" those requests. Such discrete communications mean that no continuity is recorded.

As Tom Armitage points out, because the Internet's default architecture is open or stateless, it is very good at sharing but not so good at privacy and ownership.[1] By this, he means, quite simply that "implementing state, or privacy, or ownership, or a paywall, is effort" (T. Armitage, pers. comm., February 9, 2016). State is a secondary level, patched onto a stateless system. I have to stress that this is not to say that the development and design of the Internet were free from a proprietary impetus, nor that "default" architecture is anything but conscious and intentional. My point, rather, is that at a technical level, limit-

1. Armitage made these comments during a response he gave at an event centered on James Bridle at the Whitechapel Gallery, "Systems Literacy," January 20, 2016.

ing connection and sharing on the Internet is something that has to be introduced in secondary layers and mechanisms. It also follows that tracking a user's activity has to be imposed at a secondary level. Netscape, for example, introduced the cookie—a by-now ubiquitous text file that stores small amounts of data associated with a domain. For as long as the cookie has not expired, it will track the pages a user visits and help build a user profile (see Elmer 2003). In its stateless formations, before the "effort" to impose statefulness, the Internet, then, can be conceptualized as a technology of stateless, borderless, always already sharing. I want to suggest that sharing (without tracking or remembering) in this instance is a rule conditioning the possibility of computers communicating with each other at all.

However, introducing state, tracking a user's online movements, say, foregrounds a different kind of "sharing"—one concerned no longer with open and nonaccumulative peer-to-peer communication but rather with a "sharing" of the journey, searches, and data transfers from one IP address or an individual user with the Web publisher and, often, third parties. Indeed, tech companies like Facebook and Google use the word "sharing" when referring to the monetization of users' data (see John 2013). In Instagram's 2013 privacy policy following its acquisition by Facebook, for example, there is a section titled "Sharing of Your Information."[2]

This links protocol and profits. Illegal and legal entities want a share of our data. This would include hackers should our data be interesting or profitable enough, able to overcome any data loss prevention (DLP) software and systems from firewalls to encryption. It would also include trackers utilized by Web publishers, such as DoubleClick, that log the data we

2. See https://www.instagram.com/about/legal/privacy/.

create through our online activity to customize service and advertising and sell it to third parties. Such trackers don't often announce themselves to us unless we seek them out through antitracking browser extensions (like Ghostery) or forensic examination of user agreements (which still do not list specific trackers used). Many websites have multiple trackers—cookies and beacons. Ironically, even website publishers that employ trackers are themselves subject to "data leakage," which "occurs when a brand, agency or ad tech company collects data about a website's audience and subsequently uses that data without the initial publisher's permission" (McDermott 2015). Such secretions, the unintentional "sharing" of already "shared" data, also highlight the difficulties of not sharing from a different perspective.

The idea of sharing as protocological is posited here to emphasize the fact that specific modes of sharing and not sharing, as well as the particular distribution of the (data) sensible, are determined by ideologically charged *dispositifs*. As Galloway (2004, 8) puts it, "protocol is how technological control exists after decentralization." Crucially, the conditions of sharing/not sharing today inflect a subjectivity that makes a particular call on, and imposes a limitation to, the veillant and agential capacities of citizens.

4. The Sharing Assemblage

DEPENDING ON OUR POLITICS, we will be more or less resistant to the sharing of our data in exchange for security; depending on our willingness and time to read the clauses in different privacy policies, we might be more or less cognizant of what it is, exactly, we are sharing with private corporations; depending on how much attention we paid to the details of the Snowden revelations, we will have greater or lesser understanding of the ways in which our communications and movements can be monitored by the state. Regardless of the differentials in knowledge and politics, sharing, I want to argue, has to be understood today not as a conscious and conscientious act but as a key component of contemporary data subjectivity.

Although *data* is etymologically derived from *dare*—the Latin for "to give"—it often feels as if data has been taken. This brings to mind Rob Kitchin's (2014, 2) observation that data might be better referred to as *capta* (from the Latin *capere*, "to take"). Kitchin invokes this alternative etymology to drive home the fact that data is never "raw," transparent, or objective, that it never gives itself over without the intervention of a subjective interpreter or scientist. Data has to be extracted, selected, or "taken." Whereas Kitchin, then, is thinking about the mediated, "cooked" nature of data, we can also see this tension between giving and taking in terms of subjectivity. Is our relation with data better encapsulated by giving or taking?

I would wager that neither verb quite encompasses the experience of the shareveillant data subject I am referring to. It is not clear that data belongs to us in the first place in order for it then to be given or taken. Rather, we are within a dynamic sharing assemblage: always already sharing, relinquishing data with human or nonhuman agents. I want to identify an ascendant shareveillant subjectivity that is shaped by the play between openness and enclosure. "Shareveillance" is intended to capture the condition of consuming shared data and producing data to be shared in ways that shape a subject who is at once surveillant and surveilled. To phrase it with a slightly different emphasis, the subject of shareveillance is one who simultaneously works with data and on whom the data works.

Sharing prevails as a standard of the system because of the difficulties of unsharing data and the "effort" of safeguarding or rendering data proprietary. To take the first of these, it is clear that the ease and speed of copying digital data mean that data already in circulation cannot be revoked. This has led to some farcical situations in the United Kingdom, in which information freely available on the Internet has been repressed by a super injunction within the regular press. Or consider the move in 2016 by *Pink News* to publish stories removed from search engines through Google's right-to-be-forgotten policy in the European Union (EU) that came into operation in 2014 (Duffy 2016). Although these examples pertain to information rather than data per se, the principle of digital reproduction and dissemination is the same. Moreover, in the case of cloud storage, or even backups to hard drives, replication of data is the default. More than one copy of a file often exists on a hard drive, let alone in different storage facilities. It is also pertinent to point out that it makes little sense to talk about an "original" when it comes to digital data, the consequence of which is that data is nonrivalrous and sharing nondepleting. We could also look to the way in which the use and reuse of different data sets for various applications makes it nonsensical to talk about the unsharing of data: once it is the lifeblood of various apps, bringing oxygen to a new economy, it is being shared in multiple directions through various media. We can detect, then, a propensity toward duplication, secretion, circulation, and sharing.

Sharing in commercial contexts is clearly a central part of shareveillant subjectivity. Much has been written about the commodification of users' browsing habits and metadata in the context of social media, online gaming, and the trend toward quantified self. Indeed, the idea that a user of Facebook, Twitter, Google, and so forth is not the customer but the product is commonplace today. The political economy of commercial dataveillance ensures that the activity of watching (in this case, watching not the state nor the commercial entity itself but the posts, newsfeeds, and products that have been curated by friends or algorithms) is closely aligned with sharing (with linking and liking and, at the same time, with leaving a trail to be shared with brokers and analysts who trade in big data). While I have pointed toward a distribution of the digital sensible that would encompass private and public, national and transnational, entities, in what follows, I want to focus on the ways in which state forms of "open" and "closed" data feed into such a distribution. Compared with the large amount of research on consumer dataveillance and its relationship with forms of subjectivity, relatively little research considers the demands placed on subjects by a condition of sharing in relation to the state. There are some noteworthy exceptions to this, such as Isin and Ruppert's (2015) *Being Digital Citizens,* which recognizes that "acts of sharing place unique demands on citizen subjects of cyberspace" (88). Of course, because of the level of collaboration between the state and big tech, revealed and tested by the Snowden revelations, as well as the ways those companies can sometimes challenge, exceed, transcend, or evade nation-state legislation, the distinction between government and commercial data sharing is somewhat artificial. As a consequence, I do make references to the latter in what follows, but I will focus on state practices, because they, too, can tell us much about subjectivity today.

5. Open and Closed Government Data

IT IS IMPORTANT TO NOTE from the outset that the labels "open" and "closed" are not essential but relational, adhering to particular moments in space and time. When articulated to data, the identity of each, and the binary opposition itself, is contingent on the political climate, the market, the security complex, technological capacities, and the veillant conjuncture. The tendency toward secretion identified earlier should be enough to indicate the provisional nature of any identification of data as "closed." Likewise, because of the inherently opaque nature of much "open" data (which leaves many questions unanswered, such as for whom was this data collected? To what ends?), "open" data is never simply open or transparent.

Open government data is generally understood as the provision of big and small digital data on the part of government agencies. Alongside a few critical voices (e.g., Morozov 2013), open government data is celebrated in the mainstream for democratizing knowledge distribution and research, invigorating economies, increasing efficiency, ensuring accountability, and operating as a key element in digital democracy or "Democracy 2.0" (e.g., Goldstein and Dyson 2013). Open government data is data shared with no depletion: sharing in the sense not of division but of giving multiple citizens access to the same thing.

By contrast, we can understand closed government data as that data that is withheld from public view, whether in the interests of privacy, diplomacy, or national security. As "close" brings forth etymological associations from the old French *clore,* "to shut, to cut off from," we can see how citizens are cut off from the state's data, even data they have (perhaps unknowingly) shared. In sharing this kind of data, we have in effect given it away. Our "share" can never yield. That is to say, without the interventions of whistleblowers or hackers, closed government data will never be given the opportunity to be put to uses other than those determined appropriate by the state.

In its open formation, government data is deliberately and strategically shared by the collecting agent; in its closed formation, data is deliberately and strategically not shared. With respect to closed data, particularly in the case of state surveillance, citizens share data with a proprietary agent in exchange for the privileges that come with citizenship. We might, that is, consciously or unconsciously, explicitly or implicitly, consider the collection of our GPS data or phone metadata a fair price to pay for the freedoms, benefits, and protections that come with owning a British (or Australian, German, American, etc.) passport. This pragmatic attitude to sharing with respect to closed government data, the transmission of citizens' activity to a veillant other, is echoed in the experience of digital consumers in general. That is to say, users of social media and search engines are familiar with making trade-offs between services they want and acquiescence to data collection. As well as protocological in a technological sense, then, sharing also needs to be thought as a political, cultural, and industry standard. It "frame[s] the terms and parameters by which elements of a system interact and behave" (McStay 2014, 5).

Sharing is not something we do after possessing data but is the basis on which having any relation with that data can be possible at all. All of which does not necessarily indicate that the data we have shared is digested and absorbed and immediately put to work by any surveillant agent. Rather, to borrow the words of Gus Hunt, the Central Intelligence Agency's chief technology officer, it indicates that "collect[ing] everything and hang[ing] on to it forever" (see Ingram 2013) relies on the idea that the archive is "structurally speculative" (Andrejevic and Gates 2014). The uses to which collected data will be put and the meanings it will be given are dependent on future algorithms and political concerns. This means that in a networked era, we are always already sharing without any actor in the system necessarily knowing precisely why. The principle of sharing overrides any uncertainty over the uses to which shared data can be put. Such a condition is obviously in the interests of commercial and state surveillance, which, in general, currently has monopolies on accruing economic or security value from big, aggregated archives of data.[1]

Although it might seem as though closed government data is open data's evil twin, open government data is not excluded from this veillant assemblage. All shared data mobilize a politics of visibility, a demand to align with a political and ethical distribution of the digital sensible. Though less potent and pervasive than their closed counterparts, open government data initiatives also involve veillance because the sharing of data includes a call to watch and act on that data—we are envisioned, watched, imagined as entrepreneurial and auditing viewers or subjects. Within a logic of shareveillance, both

1. It is important, of course, to acknowledge that there is also social value to be gained from sharing some big data, such as genomics and other health-related data.

closed and open data contribute to the construction of an antipoliticized data subject and public. By looking at the national security dataveillance revealed by Edward Snowden and the open government data initiatives implemented by the U.S. government, I will consider how shareveillant subjectivity is produced in the context of the state.

"Closed" Data, Securitized Veillance

The data collected by the NSA, GCHQ, and other security agencies around the globe is mostly experienced as "closed": inaccessible to those without security clearance. Before Snowden revealed the programs implemented to collect communications data and metadata—programs such as PRISM, which, since 2007, has permitted the NSA to access data from service providers, and Tempora, which saw GCHQ placing interceptors on fiber-optic cables that handle Internet traffic in and out of the United Kingdom—the programs, too, were closed, secret, opaque. That is not to say that there weren't all kinds of secretions regarding those practices: details or speculations erupting now and again into the public sphere through reportage, whistleblowing, or popular cultural representation (what Tim Melley [2012] refers to as "the covert sphere"—the representation and cultural counterpart to the covert sector). Rather than focusing on the content of the revelations and whether such news really was new, however, what I am interested in is the conceptual apparatus that was available to those who wanted to resist or challenge this aspect of the shareveillant assemblage.

Though domestic protests were subdued, calls to end the NSA's activities, as evidenced on the banners held at the march on Washington in October 2013, were expressed as an "end to mass spying."[2] Exercising people's imaginations and offending their constitutional rights was the suggestion that their own government had the ability to see them and their actions without their knowledge or explicit consent. While many would agree that this move toward ubiquitous communications surveillance is, indeed, something to resist, the appeal to "privacy" falls rather flat. Privacy is like the light we see from an already dead star. We cling to it even though we live in what our digital conjuncture has essentially rendered a postprivacy paradigm. This doesn't mean that the concept of privacy is no longer important: it still organizes legal processes, rights-based debate, and common understandings of our own sense of self. In some ways, as Andy McStay (2014, 2) points out, "many social changes since the industrial revolution involve a net increase in privacy, be this less familiarity with our neighbours, more geographically dispersed family arrangements, working away from home, weakening of religious authority . . . greater possibility of children having their own bedrooms, increase in car ownership (versus public transport)." Yet, the risk of still appealing to privacy in an era of ubiquitous dataveillance and closed, securitized data is that it reduces rather than increases political agency precisely because it misunderstands the subjectivity in question and because privacy claims are particularly weak when it comes to collective politics. It cannot, to put it in the terms to which this book adheres, redistribute the digital sensible.

To take the first of these issues, the appeal to privacy in the wake of the Snowden revelations misreads the deindividualizing character of mass covert data mining. The fear expressed on the banners and placards of the protests is that the state

2. See, for example, Reuters's (2013) footage.

sees the crowd as individuals—a mass that is made up of many Is, the privacy each of which has been infringed. The concept of privacy imagines a state violating the rights of a fully self-present liberal citizen. But the way in which data mining works means that the security services are not particularly interested in the actions of individual citizens except inasmuch as those citizens are data subjects: how they contribute to a background pattern on which an evolutionary algorithm can work to recognize minority anomalies. As Clough et al. (2014, 154) write,

> in the case of personal data, it is not the details of that data or a single digital trail that is important, but rather the relationship of the emergent attributes of digital trails en masse that allows for both the broadly sweeping and the particularized modes of affective measure and control. Big data doesn't care about "you" so much as the bits of seemingly random info that bodies generate or that they leave as a data trail.

Nova Spivack (2013), in an article infused with techno-utopianism, puts it slightly differently: "We are noise, not signal." Spivack problematically invokes this argument to excuse the NSA's data scraping (echoing the common mantra that if you have done nothing wrong, you have nothing to fear from surveillance). But we can also come to a different conclusion. The configuration of citizens as noise, not signal, points toward our delimited role within the shareveillant assemblage read from the perspective of closed data.

The offense, I suggest, is less the intrusion into private space and more the disavowal of the public as potentially political. The surveillant state imagines its citizens in this configuration as primarily an aggregated data set. It is not that citizens are being spied on that is of most concern in this view but that unless their actions are flagged up as extreme outliers, they are not considered fully formed political agents worthy of anything more than bolstering an algorithm for data analysis. To avoid peddling a fantasy about once fully agential individuals, we can invoke the idea of Michael Hardt and Antonio Negri's (2000; 2004) "multitude" (that which both emerges from Empire and has the potential to subvert this new global sovereignty). The multitude does not resemble traditional configurations but rather, as Jeremy Gilbert (2008, 164) elucidates, suggests "a field of collectivity which is composed of singularities: unique points of intersection and potential self-invention which cannot be subsumed into any simple totality nor reduced to the status of individuals." This is important because it points to an idea of political agency beyond individualism toward a distributed or networked agency. (The concept of multitude also, we should note, works from the assumption that resistance can emerge from the very same body that is seemingly invested in the perpetuation of regressive forms of power.) When the collective singularities of the multitude are translated into a data set, a hopeful reconfiguration of the political is neutralized. Rather than being of comfort, the fact that citizens only count in terms of their role as flat data has an effect on the scope of political agency to alter the distribution of the sensible (even if this is only an imagined agency) and the possibilities therein that this implies for effective, counterhegemonic collective action.

To take the second limitation of privacy—that it is a poor foundation on which to build collective action—it is one not tied to the digital/big data turn, but it is nevertheless a critique that has been given a new inflection within that context. Although it is not within the scope of this book to provide an extensive survey of work on privacy, it is worth reminding ourselves that privacy has been subject to critique from the Left for its connections with individualism, the perpetuation of oppression, and property. To call on the right to privacy is to frame the debate in terms of an individual's right to limit the access other people, the state, or commercial entities might have to her "content" (data, thoughts, feelings, information, communications) at any time. It reinforces a sense of a self that lives in political isolation. Therefore, even when people coalesce around privacy concerns, step into the light of the demos, they do so to insist on their right to step back into the apolitical shadows of individualism, away from the possibility of collective creativity or an identity-in-common. Equally, the feminist Left has challenged privacy for allowing gendered inequality and even violence to exist beyond the purview of society (e.g., MacKinnon 1989). The private sphere potentially offers respite and refuge but might be experienced more like a prison for some oppressed women. Moreover, a notion used most adeptly to protect property, privacy has been an uneasy bedfellow for collectivist leftist politics more interested in the redistribution of wealth.

In short, privacy claims are ill equipped to fundamentally challenge the dataveillance being conducted and its essentially unidirectional sharing of information that contributes to the shareveillant subjectivity I am outlining. But closed data and opaque data practices are only half of the story.

Open Data

The provision of open data is a professed concern and commitment for many liberal democracies today. The Open Government Partnership currently has seventy-five participating countries, not all of which, it should be noted, could be described as liberal democracies (the Philippines and Turkey, for example), all at various stages in implementing open government plans.[3] Though its funding was cut in 2010 from $35 million to just $8 million, and

3. See http://www.opengovpartnership.org/countries.

its future under Donald Trump is precarious to say the least, the United States's open government data portal, Data.gov, is notable in this regard, providing public access to many different data sets produced by government agencies. There are a good number of reasons to applaud transparency measures such as this, especially when compared with closed regimes in which extreme forms of corruption are endemic. And yet, this might be an inflammatory comparison, or at least a false construction of the issue. For within ostensibly "open" liberal democracies, we must ask which forms of openness take precedence in any particular era and what kinds of subjectivities they promote. Regions wishing to make the move toward more open forms of society and state often look to those *dispositifs* already in operation elsewhere, and thus forms of openness, and the political settlements they compound, travel through what I have elsewhere termed (with plenty of caveats, given the contentious nature of the latter word) "transparency imperialism" (see Birchall 2015).

In sharing its data sets with citizens, the state adds to the interpellation of shareveillant subjects. Althusser's (1971) vivid and therefore oft-quoted scenario depicting the process of becoming a subject sees a figure that responds to being hailed by a "Hey, you there!" (174). The calling policeman sees the subject, who turns to acknowledge the ideological call. The shareveillant subject is hailed with an added imperative—"Hey, you there! Come closer and watch." The subject turns not only to be seen but also to become vigilant. The shareveillant subject is surveilled (possibly without his or her knowledge, given all I have said regarding dataveillance) but also has to be seen to be seeing. More accurately, the shareveillant subject is asked to *see through*: the transparency of the state is the interface that hails us, and we cannot but occupy the position (whether we feel technically capable or not, whether we perform the function or not) of auditor, analyst, witness.

For example, on Data.gov, we are presented with an array of data sets and documents that contain statistics of varying importance in a variety of formats (CSV files, Word documents, PDFs, etc.). Watching and seeing through (and acquiring and refreshing the technological competence required to do so) become forms of immaterial labor. In the process, a characteristic of neoliberal logic is performed: the subject is bequeathed responsibility without power. He or she is given the responsibility to watch without the expertise to know what to look for nor the power to act in a meaningful way on what might be found. Echoing Max Horkheimer's (1989, 265) conclusion that the cultural industries "constantly profess their adherence to the individual's ultimate value and his inalienable freedom, but . . . operate in such a way that they tend to foreswear such values by fettering the individual to prescribed attitudes, thoughts, and buying habits," open data offers the promise of agency and freedom (of information) but shapes the scope and manifestation of those ideals to entrench shareveillance.

The act of looking, of being asked to look, is more complicated still, for even while this call to be vigilant is made, the reach widens to draw in unelected mediators: third-party application developers and data visualizers. Data entrepreneurs step into the ideological call to help fulfill the demand to watch, to see (through) the state. The "datapreneurs" happily perform this function—taking the data sets made available by the government on websites like Data.gov and turning them into user-friendly interfaces. In doing so, those datapreneurs are also, themselves, responding to a hailing: to help operationalize the new "data economy." This call manifests in different forms. The White House, under Obama, hosted "datapaloozas" on health, safety, and energy—events where datapreneurs could make contact and experiment with using open government data. In Helsinki, Finland, events called

"Helsinki Loves Developers" facilitate networking between city officials and application developers, while the city runs competitions (such as "Apps for Finland" and "Datademo") to reward Web-based or smartphone apps that use public data. The U.K. innovation agency Technology Strategy Board partially funds the Open Data Institute, the goal of which is to "train, nurture and collaborate with individuals around the world to promote innovation through open data." This is because the provision of open government data is fueled not only by its purported social value but also by its economic value.[4] In fact, in his foreword to "Open Data White Paper: Unleashing the Potential," presented to the U.K. Parliament in 2012, the Right Honorable Francis Maude mentions "demonstrating the value of open governance to economic growth" before "improved citizen engagement and empowerment" (5) when explaining the priorities of the British chairmanship of the Open Data Partnership, which goes under the heading "Transparency Drives Prosperity."

The data economy is earmarked to stimulate and fuel economies, with some impressive potential figures being cited. For example, a report by the McKinsey Global Institute from 2013 estimates that the global market in open data, measured in terms of job creation, profit margins, and efficiency savings, is worth up to $5 trillion a year. The World Bank (2014, 20) finishes its own macroeconomic report on the value of open data by stating, "While sources differ in their precise estimates of the economic potential of Open Data, all are agreed that it is potentially very large." Though these two reports are not lim-

---

4. Of course, this blurring of the social and economic is a key characteristic of the Internet. Thus social media platforms present their product as performing a service to, or even creating, a community (see Turner 2006).

ited to open *government* data, a report from the Open Data Institute (2015) analyzing various reports on the value of open data tells us that "those studies focused on the value of public sector open data alone found that it is worth between 0.4% and 1.5% of an economy's GDP."

The datapreneur is the key figure in the success of the (open) data economy, as the actor who must harness the potential of the data to create value from raw data sets. That could include the team behind Zocdoc, an app that uses data from the U.S. Census Bureau and the Centers for Medicare and Medicaid Services to assist patients as they manage the complex system of U.S. health insurance and provision, or the datapreneurs behind Spotcrime, an app that again uses U.S. census data, but this time to produce a searchable map that contains crime statistics for each area. In the United Kingdom, the Findthebest website uses the open census and Department of Education data on Data.gov.uk to produce searchable league tables on primary and secondary schools with information as detailed as average teacher's salary and the distribution of a school's budget. For the state and datapreneur alike, data is configured as a resource ripe for mining and commodification.

Where does this leave the shareveillant subject? At once asked to watch the newly transparent state, with all its data organs on display, and to rely on the mediating and translating functions of datapreneurs to do so, this subject is one whose relationship to government is shaped by the market. Neoliberal ideology has long ensured the public acquiescence to and accommodation of the marketization of many aspects of social and political life, from education to health. What is new here is that the market (embodied by third-party datapreneurs) gets to decide the very stakes of the political—and many apps made possible by Data.gov and Data.gov.uk are concerned with real estate, finding the best school or surgeon, checking food safety statistics, transport information, and weather data.[5] They help citizens navigate a variable field of provision rather than evening out that field (by, for example, implicitly encouraging people to avoid underperforming schools rather than ensuring that those schools receive more assistance). I am arguing that the reliance on data mediators or datapreneurs to make the transparency of the state meaningful means that, ultimately, the market determines the distribution of the sensible—what we can know, see, hear, touch, encounter. In terms of sharing, only those data sets that can be made to yield profit (in some form) will be shared in such a format that the data can be received, understood, and rendered actionable.

The shareveillant subject is required to be vigilant and veillant to be a fully engaged citizen. Immediately, however, this impossible vigilance of the open state is acknowledged, and mediators are called on to select and package information. This means that veillance is always watchfulness, not of the fully transparent state, but of selected mediations brought forth. Transparency is obscured by its own impossible glare—only the data that the market has primed us to want (usually data that can help us make apparently "informed" choices in a complex public–private landscape) assume the face of state transparency in the data economy. The risk is that it becomes increasingly difficult to participate in and navigate the state outside of these commodified, shaped, and edited forms of aggregated data. What kind of "control" is in play here?

5. It is important to recognize that this is not the whole story. There are, for example, some potentially revealing apps made possible by freely available data that highlight possible connections between donations and votes (e.g., Greenhouse at http://allaregreen.us). Having said this, in his article "Against Transparency," Lawrence Lessig (2009) provides a scathing critique even of apps that try to illustrate the link between votes and donations.

Gilles Deleuze's (1992) short but influential essay "Postscript on the Societies of Control" offers a reading of power, governmentality, and political economy in postdisciplinary societies that can help here. In the "Postscript," Deleuze evokes Foucault's work on discrete and autonomous units of confinement characteristic of disciplinary societies to establish more contemporaneous dispersed mechanisms of control. Data-driven government transparency, which as a move from administrative to democratic accountability might seem like an unequivocal good, can be problematized through Deleuze's societies of control to give a clear sense of why techniques of emancipation can be experienced otherwise.

Although Deleuze's essay predates by several decades the data-driven government transparency on which this book focuses, it can help us to understand this phenomenon in a number of ways. First, just as Deleuze identifies the way in which environments of enclosures (like the prison, the hospital, and the school) are now subject to forms of free-floating control, we can see how, in opening up government, making (some of) its boundaries porous through open data, outsourcing, and responsibilization, data-driven transparency ensures that the business of governance (and citizenship) is without boundaries or end. So while government becomes "smaller" in many ways, to allow the market to do much of the work previously accorded the state, government simultaneously has a ubiquitous presence in the form of raw data or, perhaps more important, digital tools to help navigate the state in its market form. Like the corporation, which has replaced the factory, data-driven government transparency makes government "a spirit, a gas" (4).

Second, through Deleuze's observation that control mechanisms are inseparable variations, we can see open data and the data economy in relation to other "modulations" (4) in the neoliberal field. As opposed to enclosures, which are molds or castings, modulations are "like a self-deforming cast that will continuously change from one moment to the other" (4). Modulations are "in states of perpetual metastability that operate through challenges, contests" (4). The data economy as an entrepreneurial enterprise, in which open data plays a crucial role, necessarily requires such metastability to become profitable. Moreover, datapaloozas and hackathons are clear examples of the "challenges" and "contests" that drive remuneration and profit. Crucially, the logic of control means that each experience of governmentality is a continuity. Open data is thus one modulation within a "continuous network" (6) that demands perpetual vigilance and innovation.

Third, in a formulation that helps us assess what is at stake in the technological conditions of open data, Deleuze shows that we can be controlled through the conditions of access and confinement. He cites Félix Guattari's example of an electronic card that can open barriers in a city but that "could just as easily be rejected on a given day or between certain hours; what counts is not the barrier but the computer that tracks each person's position—licit or illicit—and effects a universal modulation" (7). The emancipatory qualities of open data involve control because of the entrepreneurial metastasis required to convert a previously extraeconomic form into capital, the continuous vigilance of data subjects, submission to market logic as a form that can determine the scope of the political, and forms of dataveillance that track and trace.

It would be an exaggeration to claim that Deleuze is nostalgic about the certainties of disciplinary societies, but it is fair to say that environments of enclosure with their clear borders offer more opportunities for distinctive, oppositional subject positions or the creation of counterpublics. While not using disciplinary societies as her reference point, Jodi Dean (2009, 51) writes, "Whereas the Keynesian welfare state interpellated subjects into specific symbolic identities (such as the worker, the housewife, the student or the citizen), neoliberalism relies on imaginary identities. Not only do the multiplicity and variability of such identities prevent them from serving as loci of political action but their inseparability from the injunctions of consumerism reinforces capitalism's grip." In general, the neoliberal subject is "one who strategizes for her- or himself among various social, political and economic options, not one who strives with others to alter or organize these options" (Brown 2005, 43). Even armed with the information provided through open data, the shareveillant subject, specifically, is a precarious position from which to enact or coalesce counterhegemonies because it is reliant on continuing the forms of control to which it is subjected. That is to say, the shareveillant subject has learned to experience and accept agency and subjectivity via the forms of veillance and sharing described in this book.

6. Interrupting Shareveillance: New Cuts

> There is no need to fear or hope, but only to look for new weapons.
>
> —GILLES DELEUZE, "Postscript on the Societies of Control"

THE SHAREVEILLANT SUBJECT, then, is rendered politically impotent from (at least) two, not necessarily distinct, directions. In the face of state and commercial dataveillance, the subject's choices (whether with whom to communicate, what to circulate, or what to buy) are compulsorily shared to contribute to an evolving algorithm to make advertising, say, or governmentality more efficient, targeted, precise. The public is configured as rich big data rather than as a network of singularities with resistant potential. Open government portals share the state's data with subjects and, in doing so, responsibilize and isolate individuals and thus disavow the legitimacy of collective power. In addition, this form of accountability produces a limited relation with the information provided. In monitoring the granular transactions of government—in the form of U.K. MPs' expenses, for example, now available online after the scandal of 2009,[1] or the White House's visitor's log, financial disclosures, and annual reports to Congress, also offered online

1. http://www.mpsallowance.parliament.uk.

during the Obama administration[2]—the armchair auditor is only permitted to spot anomalies or aberrations in a system he or she has to otherwise acknowledge as fair. This form of sharing, of openness, anticipates a limited form of engagement and response. And, as I have outlined, even this armchair auditor able to engage with "raw" data is largely a fiction produced by the rhetoric of open government; the crucial role that datapreneurs and app developers play in mediating data means that the state's sharing and the citizen's share of the state are subject to market forces.

I want to reiterate that I am not imagining a once fully agential political subject who has now been supplanted by this shareveillant version, compromised by marketized, securitized, and neoliberal apparatus such as algorithmic governmentality and open data portals. Political agency has always been limited by structural and relational conditions as well as the fluidity, fragmentation, or fracture of psyches and subjectivities. Nevertheless, the particular discursive–material conditions that curtail agency alongside those other inescapable metaphysical limitations matter. For it is from here that we can more fully understand the singularity of the particular distribution we face.

It is one thing, of course, to diagnose a condition and quite another to prescribe a remedy. If one accepts that shareveillance supports a political settlement not conducive to radical equality, and that a more equitable distribution is something to strive for, how might shareveillance be interrupted? I would like to offer one possible strategy, while recognizing that there will be, and need to be, others. The conceptual framework for my interruption is inspired by the etymology of *share*. From

2. https://www.whitehouse.gov/briefing-room/disclosures.

the Old English *scearu*—"a cutting, shearing, tonsure; a part or division"—the root of the meaning of *share* apropos "portion," to the term *scear,* with respect to plowshare, meaning, simply, "that which cuts," cutting clearly resonates within the concept and practice of sharing.

This focus is certainly supported by Rancière's (2004a, 225) framing of the distribution of the sensible, at least in certain translations:

> I understand by this phrase the cutting up [*decoupage*] of the perceptual world that anticipates, through its sensible evidence, the distribution of shares and social parties. . . . And this redistribution itself presupposes a cutting up of what is visible and what is not, of what can be heard and what cannot, of what is noise and what is speech.

What share we have of resources, as well as the mode of sharing, falls along the lines of a particular distribution or cut. The way we share, the conditions and decisions underlying how and what we share, what I am calling the "cut," create a certain distribution. My focusing in on the term *cut* here is, as I've confessed, inspired by the etymological roots of *share,* but I am also mindful of Sarah Kember and Joanna Zylinska's (2012) productive use of it in *Life after New Media.* Thinking about mediation as a "complex and hybrid process" that is "all-encompassing and indivisible" (Kember and Zylinksa 2012, xv), the authors draw on a range of thinkers, including Henri Bergson, Karen Barad, Jacques Derrida, and Emmanuel Levinas, to imagine cuts (into the temporality of mediation) as creative, ethical incisions and decisions. Thus photography, to take their most potent example, is

> understood here as a process of cutting through the flow of mediation on a number of levels: perceptive, material, technical, and conceptual. The recurrent moment of the cut—one we are familiar with not just via photography but also via film making,

sculpture, writing, or, indeed, any other technical practice that involves transforming matter—is posited here as both a technique (an ontological entity encapsulating something that is, or something that is taking place) and an ethical imperative (the command: "Cut!"). (xvii–xix)

This leads Kember and Zylinska to ask what it means to "cut well" (xix). It is a question that every artist must ask himself or herself and practice, they argue. This imperative to cut well extends to all acts of mediation (any other technical practice that involves transforming matter), including the kinds of practices that mediate data that I engage with in this book. Obviously, not everyone who works with data is an "artist" in the way we would traditionally understand that term. But if we draw on aesthetics in the Rancièrean sense—as a distributive regime that determines political possibilities—then we can begin to see different decisions being made as to how and when to cut into data and what to reveal or conceal about that decision-making process itself, as ethical or unethical.

When we are cut off from our data (as is the case with closed data), we are not given the opportunity to make our own cuts *into* it. Equally, if the cut *of* data is such that we can only engage with the data in ways that support a political settlement we might not agree with—if what might appear as an ethical provision of data (through transparency measures, for example) in fact supports or makes more efficient an unethical system—then our cuts are determined with strict parameters. To cut (and therefore share) differently, to cut against the grain, we have to interrupt the strictures of shareveillance.

Many interruptive cuts deserve to be mentioned. First, by not abiding by the rules of privatized and securitized access and copyright laws, some acts of hacking can highlight the unidirectional sharing of closed data and systems. Bracketing off those hackers who are recruited by intelligence agencies and

cybersecurity firms, independent hackers could be character-
ized as performing guerilla sharing (of source code, access,
software, recovered data), taking a share where none was offered. Second, decentralized data storage facilities like Storj[3]
and SAFE[4] offer distributed object storage across the network,
utilizing excess hard drive space, as an alternative to traditional cloud storage solutions (what Geert Lovink [2016, 11] calls
"centralized data silos"). By employing peer-to-peer technologies to distribute data across nodal points, this new kind of
cloud computing shares out encrypted data in a way that interrupts the flow of data upstream to surveillant third parties.
Third, and this leads on from the previous example, encryption
technologies delimit sharing communities by requiring keys
for decryption; sharing is, therefore, more controlled. Far from
being an unconscious default, sharing becomes a purposeful
and targeted action. Take, for example, the "off-the-record"
encryption used by the free and open source instant messaging application Adium, favored by journalists and nongovern-
mental organization workers. According to the Off-the-Record
Development Team, this technology offers not only encryption
of instant messaging and authentication of your correspond-
ent's identity but also deniability, because the messages one
sends do not have digital signatures that can be checked by a
third party, and what they call "forward secrecy," which means
that if the user loses control of his or her private keys, no previous conversation is compromised.[5]

Some of the most creative cuts into shareveillance can
be encapsulated by the term *data obfuscation.* In their book

3. https://storj.io/.
4. http://maidsafe.net/.
5. See https://adium.im/help/pgs/AdvancedFeatures
-OTREncryption.html.

Obfuscation: A User's Guide for Privacy and Protest, Finn Brunton and Helen Nissenbaum (2015, 1) identify a number of different obfuscation strategies that demonstrate a "deliberate addition of ambiguous, confusing, or misleading information to interfere with surveillance and data collection." Brunton and Nissenbaum consider, among other technologies, the Onion Router (TOR), which allows for online anonymity through the combined tactics of encrypting communication and relaying it via several nodes on the Internet to obscure the source and destination; TrackMeNot, a browser extension that floods search engines with random search terms to render algorithms ineffective; and the privacy plug-in FaceCloak, which encrypts genuine information offered to Facebook so that it can only be viewed by other friends who also use FaceCloak.

We could also add to their examples tracking blockers like Ghostery, which intervene in consumer dataveillance by alerting users to, and in some cases disabling, cookies, tags, and beacons, and search engines like DuckDuckGo and StartPage, which allow for online searching without being tracked or profiled as with facilities like Google Search, the business model of which relies on the accumulation of consumer and user profiles and browsing habits. While driven by privacy concerns and corporate confidentiality, the Blackphone developed by Silent Circle offers mobile users a mode of communication built on a concept other than the form of sharing figured by shareveillance. Aptly, one of the professed unique selling propositions of the phone is that it is "built on a fundamentally different protocol."[6] The online promotional video[7] consists of a series of interviews with mobile users (or actors posing as mobile users)

6. https://www.silentcircle.com/products-and-solutions/technology/.

7. https://www.silentcircle.com/our-story/.

who are asked to read out the terms and conditions of use of the apps on their mobile phones. One woman stumbles on the fact that she has agreed to an app being able to change her call log. A man realizes he has given an app permission to record audio at any time without his confirmation. A woman is incredulous that an app can "modify calendar events and send e-mails without [her] knowledge." Yet another mobile user looks concerned that an app can read his text messages and modify his contacts. To back away from what Google's Eric Schmidt called "the creepy line" and prevent leaky data, Blackphone uses its own operating system, offers compartmentalization facilities between work and social life in a way that goes against the grain of Facebook's integrated philosophy and "real-name" policy, and preloads apps to "put you in control of what you share."[8] Crucially, the Blackphone, like the other technologies described earlier, interrupts and asks us to question default modes of digital sharing.

Owen Campbell-Moore offers a playful cut into shareveillance in the form of a Chrome extension he devised during his time at Oxford University. Using a technique known as JPEG steganography, Secretbook enables users to hide messages in photos on Facebook by making many visually imperceptible changes to encode the secret data.[9] Traditionally complex, steganography tools are simplified and therefore democratized by Campbell-Moore. Here the act of sharing a photograph on and "with" Facebook belies another, more targeted sharing: one that requires any receiver to have a password. Messages are thus hidden not only from other Facebook users but also from Facebook's scanning algorithms and profile-building analytics.

---

8. https://www.silentcircle.com/products-and-solutions/devices/.
9. See https://chrome.google.com/webstore/detail/secretbook /plglafijddgpenmohgiemalpcfgjjbph?hl=en-GB.

Whereas cryptography can flag up encoded communications to surveillant entities, steganography (within a platform like Facebook, which has to deal with more than 350 million photos being uploaded every day) has more chance of slipping secret messages through unnoticed.[10]

Galloway and Thacker (2007) describe such tactics and technologies as affording nonexistence—a chance to be "unaccounted for," not because the subject is hiding, but because she is invisible to a particular screen. They write, "One's data is there, but it keeps moving, of its own accord, in its own temporary autonomous ecology" (135). Although it could be argued that such interruptive cuts into shareveillance are isolated and therefore limited in scope, "the very oppressive pervasiveness of capitalist realism means that even glimmers of alternative political and economic possibilities can have a disproportionately great effect" (Fisher 2009, 80–81).

As a particularly decisive cut that utilizes obfuscation to show the perils of sharing qua open data, I will briefly outline a project published in 2016 by artist Paolo Cirio called *Obscurity*.[11] In the United States, the publication of police photographs, or "mug shots," of arrestees is legal under Freedom of Information and transparency laws in most states. Websites scrape mug shots that have been published elsewhere, mostly on sites belonging to law enforcement entities, and republish the photographs, requesting money from the arrestee to remove the picture and details. In *Obscurity*, Cirio and his collaborators

10. Campbell-Moore (2013) does admit that "the goal of this project was to demonstrate a proof of concept of performing steganography on a social network with JPEG recompression, not to provide total security. Hence this application is only suitable for casual users and is totally useless for serious applications such as terrorism since detection would not be difficult for organisations such as the NSA."

11. See https://obscurity.online.

have developed a program to clone and scramble the data available on mug shot industry websites, such as MugShots.com, JustMugShots.com, and MugShotsOnline.com. Using almost identical domain names to these sites, Cirio's clone sites show hazy faces that are impossible to identify and names that have been changed. Although Cirio is most concerned with the right to be forgotten, as the issue has come to be referred to in the EU after the landmark case in 2014 that ensured search engines like Google are subject to the existing EU data protection directive, we can also read this project as one that exposes the risks (of abuse and exploitation) inherent to "sharing" and the limits and failures of some open data or transparency initiatives. In addition, with the concerns of the current book in mind, the mug shot industry can be thought of as aping, cynically and darkly, the work undertaken by datapreneurs to transform open data into profitable forms. After all, the websites Cirio is protesting against indeed have an entrepreneurial, creative approach to repurposing open data.

By cutting into shareveillance, Cirio demands that incarceration be seen not as a decontextualized, individualized problem but as a collective, social issue for which we all have responsibility. He writes (Cirio, n.d.), "Obscurity proposes a democratic judicial system that would help to understand crime as a community-related issue, bringing attention to the victims of mass incarceration in the US and the unscrupulous criminal justice system and law enforcement agencies that created this situation." The project exposes the unethical cut of shareveillance with respect to a particular sociopolitical issue: how, in this case, mug shot websites share data in such a way that presents incarceration as an asocial issue, while in the process performing a second tier of punishment (shaming and extortion) on top of any lawfully imposed penalties. The project asks us to see incarceration in terms of the political economy as well as the stratified and stratifying nature of the carceral state. It cuts into this particular distribution to share anew. Creative interruptions of shareveillance can make ethical cuts and, in the process, show up the incisions that have constructed the neoliberal securitized settlement of which shareveillant subjectivity is a part.

As well as the digital and aesthetic experiments with obfuscation outlined earlier, cutting into or interrupting shareveillance might include

- imagining forms of transparency that do not simply make already inequitable systems more efficient
- not using the morally inflected language of sharing when it comes to personal data (see Prainsack 2015)—it's not always "good" to share (despite what we tell children)
- acknowledging the unconditional secret and insisting on a right to opacity rather than privacy

To help with the last of these, I turn to the thought of Jacques Derrida and Édouard Glissant.

Derrida (2001) professed a "taste for the secret." Rather than the common, contextual secret that hides somewhere waiting to be revealed (the secret that is, in principle at least, knowable), the secret of Derrida's (1992, 201) formulation is the unconditional secret: "an experience that does not make itself available to information." It is not unknowable because it is enigmatic but because knowledge, an event, a person, or a thing, is not fully present. That is, in any communication, any expression of knowledge, something is always "held back." What is "held back" is in no way held in a reserve, waiting to be discovered. Rather, there is a singular excess that cannot fully come forth. In this sense, there will always be something secret. It is an undepletable excess that defies not only the surface/depth model and its promise that truth can be revealed but also the attendant metaphysics of presence. Eschewing the hermeneutic drive and circumventing attempts to anticipate revelation, the unconditional secret within a text should be thought of as an encounter with the Other through which a responsibility of reading is made possible (and, it is important to note, if we are to take proper account of Derrida's aporia, impossible).

The secret here is best understood within the realm of ethics. Extending this ethical concern, the role of the secret in democracy leads Derrida (2001, 59) to defend the secret qua singularity, seeing it as an alternative to "the demand that everything be paraded in the public square." "If a right to the secret is not maintained," he writes, "we are in a totalitarian space" (59). This is also the logic underpinning Byung-Chul Han's (2015) recent book *The Transparency Society,* in which he claims, "Transparency is an ideology. Like all ideologies, it has a positive core that has been mystified and made absolute. The danger of transparency lies in such ideologization. If totalized, it yields terror" (viii). For Derrida (1996, 81), real democracy has to allow for secrets/singularities. If democracy is to be meaningful, it must play host to multiple singularities, including those who do not wish to respond, participate in, or belong to the public sphere. More than this, democracy is nothing but the play between openness and secrecy, between belonging and nonbelonging, sharing and not sharing. In taking account of singularities in this way, democracy, for Derrida, is always "to come." It is an impossible project: true democracy would create belonging among people who will never belong.

In light of such a formulation, we should be concerned for those who do not want to adhere to the dominant doctrines of digital democracy, including the ascendant principles of transparency, veillance, and sharing. The subject of democracy is not simply one who is asked to be transparent to the state and act on transparency. He or she is also, in the guise of Derrida's nonself-present subject, one who is constituted by a singularity, an unconditional secret, that prevents full capitulation to the demands of transparency and sharing.

In a very different context to the one I am engaged with, but drawing on Derrida's thought, Glissant coined the term a "right to opacity." Glissant was writing about an ontological condition of minoritarian subjectivity and r(el)ationality that resists the demand to be knowable, understood, and rendered transparent by the dominant, Western, filial-based order (Glissant 2011): readable within the racialized terms already set by the dominant group. This means not settling for an idea of "difference" as the basis of an ethical relation to the Other but pushing further toward recognition of an irreducible opacity or singularity (Glissant 1997, 190). For Glissant, opacity is the "foundation of Relation and confluence" (190). What is important for the current study is the way in which the ethical subject is more aligned with secrecy than transparency in Glissant's writing. Such a configuration offers us an alternative to the idea of the "good" shareveillant subject of neoliberalism.

While respecting the origins of these concepts in philosophical work on democracy and literature with respect to Derrida, and race with respect to Glissant, they can provide inspiration for thinking through the concerns of this book. Derrida's unconditional secret highlights the unethical violation (against singularity) at the heart of shareveillant practices, while a right to opacity in the context I am concerned with would mean the demand not to be reduced to, understood as, consume, and share data in ways defined by state or consumer shareveillance. Rather than with acts of publicity, such as legal marches or online petitions, I want to argue that we need to meet the pervasive protocols of inequitable dataveillance employed by the securitized state and the logic of shareveillance with forms of illegibility: a reimagined opacity. Such reformulations of the politics of the secret and opacity enable us to begin to rethink the role of sharing in a data ecology that demands visible, surveillable, quantifiable, and entrepreneurial subjects.

The identity of the shareveilled data object–neoliberal data subject cum data set is not one that is allowed to interact with data in the creation or exploration of radical collective politics. A right to opacity could be mobilized to refuse the shareveillant distribution of the digital sensible. It might offer an opportunity to formulate a politics based not on privacy but on opacity; rather than a permanent and wholesale rejection of, or retreat from, the idea and practice of sharing (data, for our concerns), opacity used in this context would only ever be desirable if it allowed space to develop community-forming openness based on the principle of "commons" rather than its shareveillant manifestation. The commons is a multifaceted term that "can be seen as an intellectual framework and political philosophy; . . . a set of social attitudes and commitments; . . . an experiential way of being and even a spiritual disposition; . . . an overarching worldview" (Bollier and Helfrich 2012). But in all of these framings of commons and commoning, questions of *what* is shared and *how* come to the fore (de Angelis 2007, 244) in a way that places into question the logic of the shareveillant settlement. In other words, it is not only the enclosure, commodification, and privatization of previously communal or community-owned natural resources, land, property, goods, services, or relations that the concept of commons challenges but also the particular shape, place, and role sharing is given in any society. As an alternative to the shareveillant subject, then, we could propose a "common subject." As Silvia Federici (2012) emphasizes,

> if commoning has any meaning, it must be the production of ourselves as a common subject. This is how we must understand the slogan "no commons without community." But "community" has to be intended not as a gated reality, a grouping of people joined

by exclusive interests separating them from others, as with communities formed on the basis of religion or ethnicity, but rather as a quality of relations.

The common subject and the opaque subject are not in opposition: both, rather, interrupt the (at least in the contemporary conjuncture) pervasive interpellation of shareveillance. They offer other vantage points from which to make cuts into the distribution of the sensible and salvage a concept of sharing. For Geert Lovink (2016, 12), this is one of a series of revisions that needs to take place if we are to achieve a "cooperative renaissance of the Internet" revolving around "organized networks" that can allow us to think outside of "the 'like' economy and its weak links. Mutual aid outside the recommendation industry. Sharing outside of Airbnb and Uber."

7. Working with Opacity

IT IS NOT a case of deciding whether to accept open data as a compensation for opaque data collection practices and closed data but of understanding the different ways in which all are part of the shareveillant logic of digital governmentality, recognizing the new epistemological and ontological calls made on shareveillant subjects and attempting to imagine and create new spaces of sharing beyond this logic.

To think about what a non-shareveillant version of sharing might look like, I will close by considering an ethicopolitical engagement with sharing in a particular context: that of academic publishing. In doing so, I will address the implications of a reassessment of sharing, openness, and opacity for academics. Such implications would include, for a start, thinking more critically about what kinds of publishing, networks, and communication we want to develop if we are guided by a right to opacity or an appropriated idea of sharing rather than the forms of openness supported by shareveillance. If, for a moment, we consider the idea of appropriating openness and sharing, where might open access, so quickly becoming a required component of the academic's publishing plans, fit into this?

Gary Hall (2008) has tirelessly challenged standard ways of conceptualizing open access while applying the tenets of open access in more radical ways. For example, he remarks on the way in which open access is mostly envisaged and discussed in terms of how it augments scholarly publishing in traditional codex books (and, consequently, the way in which scholarly disciplines are imagined and organized):

> [Open access] is understood largely in terms of providing an increase in the amount of material that can be stored, the number of people who have access to it, the potential impact of that material, the range of distribution, the ease of information retrieval, reductions in staffing, production and reproduction costs and so forth. The argument then usually focuses on whether different aspects of this transformation can be considered to be a "good" or a "bad" thing. (10)

To move the debate about digital open access on, Hall calls for a rigorous consideration of how the unfixed and ephemeral nature of digital texts, and "their undermining of the boundaries separating authors, editors, producers, users, consumers, humans and machines," and their ability to include and fuse sound, still, and moving images "contain the potential, not merely to remediate older media forms, and thus deliver a pre-existing and more-or-less unchanged content, albeit in a new way, but to transform fundamentally that content, and with it our relationship to knowledge" (10). Therefore there might not be anything particularly or inherently radical about sharing knowledge through open access (even if this is more desirable than knowledge silos). What is radical about digital open access texts is that they have the potential to intervene in politico-institutional pressures placed on cultural production and alter ideological assumptions about what a text and an author can and should do and mean.

To experiment with such possibilities, Hall and I collaborated on two series of online "books." The first was named *Liquid*

Books and the second *Living Books about Life*.[1] The books were made available on both a *gratis* (free) and a *libre* (reuse) basis. Whereas the first is a more common incarnation of academic sharing, the second is more contentious "despite the fact that the ability to *re-use* material is actually an essential feature of what has become known as the Budapest-Bathesda-Berlin (BBB) definition of open access, which is one of the major agreements underlying the movements" (Adema and Hall 2013, 152). In addition to being available to read and reuse, users of the *Liquid* and *Living* books have the opportunity to re-edit, rewrite, annotate, translate, and add to them in a shared, distributed, or networked model of authorship/curatorship. As the books link to and organize other open access materials across the Internet, users can offer new links or reorganize the existing links into new themes. Such plasticity is enabled by the wiki platform we employed. As an intervention into monetized forms of academic sharing qua publishing, on one hand, and accepted forms of sharing in the guise of standard open access, on the other, it was crucial that these books be open on a read/write basis. In this instance, a reevaluation of sharing, by pushing open access to its limits, prompts self-examination on the part of scholars as to our role and investment in knowledge production, intellectual property, notions of authorship, and the political economy of circulation and distribution.

But the implications for scholars might also lead to different kinds of experiments. We might think it more productive

1. *Liquid Books* can be found at http://liquidbooks.pbworks.com /w/page/11135951/FrontPage, *Living Books About Life* at http://www .livingbooksaboutlife.org/. The other series editor for the *Living Books about Life* project was Joanna Zylinska, and members of the project team included Sigi Jöttkandt, David Ottina, and Pete Woodbridge.

to explore the productive possibilities of obfuscation and opacity, in addition to openness and sharing. As well as looking to the thought of Derrida and Glissant for conceptual inspiration on opacity, we can also draw on the tactical politico-aesthetic imagination of two collectives from different ends of the twentieth century: Acéphale (1936–39) and Tiqqun (1999–2001). Disgusted with politics, even revolutionary politics, which he considered to be too swayed by the promise and spoils of power, Georges Bataille wanted a community invested, rather, in freedom, and he thought the best way to do this was through a secret society (as well as its public counterparts, the publication that shared Acéphale's name [Bataille 1997] and the Collège de Sociologie). Bataille wanted to "use secrecy as a weapon rather than a retreat" (Lütticken 2006, 32) while he imagined how his secret society Acéphale (which translates as "Headless") could regenerate or revolutionize society at large by privileging expenditure, risk, and loss. He sought out the shadows, that is, not as an act of disengagement but to enable him to enact a metaphorical and literal decapitation to suppress reason and release the energy of living things (Bataille 1991). Opacity here is envisaged as a generative state that can produce possibilities, affects, and effects.

In its "Cybernetic Hypothesis," the collective Tiqqun ([2001] 2009), which was highly influenced by Bataille, among others, calls for "interference," "haze," or "fog" as the "prime vector of revolt." Tiqqun prophetically saw opacity as a means to challenge the political project of cybernetics and "the tyranny of transparency which control imposes." Tiqqun itself, which published between 1999 and 2001, opted for collective anonymity and distributed authorial agency over individual publicity. After its dissolution, some members went on to write and work under the equally anonymous Invisible Committee. (In fact, though the Invisible Committee chose to operate under the auspices of opacity, the arrest of some of its members in 2008 under the charge of domestic terrorism quickly placed them under an unwelcome spotlight.[2])

While we may or may not align with the animating philosophies behind these experimental secret societies and anonymous collectives, and we have to take into account the very different historical conditions within which each existed, it is important to recognize the way in which opacity provides cover in order to share scholarship, theories, and revolutionary politics, in ways that avoid certain traps of incorporation, traditional understandings of authorship (and ownership), and/or the surveillant capacities of the state.

While these projects could be accused of eccentric whimsy, their (serious) play with opacity, with making ethical decisions about what and when to share, what and when to hold back, has resonance for anyone working in the neoliberal, audit culture of the contemporary university (I am particularly thinking of the U.K. context, but the experiences will be familiar to academics elsewhere, to a greater or lesser extent).

The institutional experience of the modern British academic includes logging and tracking time through the Transparent Approach to Costing (TRAC) Time Allocation Survey (TAS); having annual performance reviews in which one's output is accounted for and goals set; having lectures recorded by Lecture Capture; having student feedback aggregated and collated; being assessed in the National Student Survey; having one's institution ranked in various league tables; and, most notoriously, being subject to the auditing practices of the Research Excellence Framework and, now, the Teaching Excellence Framework. Obviously, the rise of audit culture in British universities is not

2. See Smith (2010) for an account of Tiqqun, the Invisible Committee, and the arrests of the "Tarnac 9."

a neutral process but has accompanied "the transformation of the traditional liberal and Enlightenment idea of the university as a place of higher learning into the modern idea of the university as corporate enterprise whose primary concern is with market share, servicing the needs of commerce, maximizing economic return and investment, and gaining competitive advantage in the 'Global Knowledge Economy'" (Shore 2008, 282). In constantly reminding ourselves of this manifestation of neoliberalism, it becomes clear that our acquiescence to these processes of audit is a political matter.

Sara Ahmed (2010) writes about her experience of this culture and the resulting necessity of knowing when to keep silent and when to keep certain things out of sight. In circumstances when speaking and revealing can be co-opted by empty rhetoric rather than ethics, silence and obfuscation are strategies of resistance and displays of resilience. To illustrate, she recalls her involvement with producing a race equality action plan for her university at the behest of the Race Relations Amendment Act of 2001. Though she took great care to avoid writing a "happy diversity document" (xviii) and, rather, foregrounded whiteness as institutional, because the document was deemed "excellent," the vice-chancellor interpreted this as meaning the university was succeeding in terms of racial equality. She reminds us that "documents that aim to reveal can be used to conceal what they reveal" (xviii). Consequently, Ahmed invokes the figure of the secretary to symbolize the need for discretion and secretion:

> [A] secretary is one who is entrusted with secrets. Sometimes we need to keep the secrets and be worth this trust. Sometimes we need not to keep the secrets with which we are entrusted even if this means we become untrustworthy. What we do with what we are entrusted—whether we speak or keep silent—remains an important question. (xx)

The secretary, therefore, is a model for anyone who sees himself or herself as having to make a decision about when sharing in institutional settings reinforces a politics that does not offer an equitable distribution of the sensible. Sharing, that is, suggests equitability and democratization, but shares are not equally distributed in shareveillance, and access to data is compromised by certain conditions of access and the necessity for mediation or translation. At times, we will need to demand meaningful, contextualized transparency about auditing measures carried out under the guise of progressive transparency. At others, we may need to employ collective withdrawal from a *dispositif* that binds us. A right to opacity means, here, the right to refrain from sharing in, and being understood according to, a distribution we may not support.

Alongside adopting a radical approach to open access, experimenting with opacity as a means to share ideas, and employing politicized discretion in the institutional setting of the university, what else can academics do to "cut well": deciding when, where, and how to share; when to be guided by an ethic of openness; and when to affirm a right to opacity even in the act of research and analysis? At various points, this could include any of the following: not placing too much faith in revelation or exposé alone; contextualizing and problematizing invocations of openness and transparency; intervening in, rather than accepting, dominant conditions of visibility; or pushing beyond ideology critique, or what Eve Kosofsky Sedgwick (2003) famously called "paranoid reading," while still being attuned to the opaque operations and erasures of discursive power.

In this reattunement of our scholarship and practice, and the echoes it can have beyond the university, closure can be reimagined as a productive opacity, and sharing can be repoliticized through understanding it as a series of decisions and cuts. In a conjuncture that places a premium on the know-ability and surveillability of subjects, in which everyone must share his or her data, come forth and be understood as data, these experiments and imaginative cuts become ethical, po-litical acts.

Afterword: Trumping Shareveillance

AT THE TIME of finishing this manuscript (June 2017), Donald Trump has been in the White House for only five months. Exactly how his administration will deal with open and closed data and the surveillant capacities of the state is still unfolding. With regard to dataveillance, Trump chose a CIA director (Mike Pompeo) and an attorney general (Jeff Sessions) sympathetic to the restoration of Section 215 of the USA PATRIOT Act that, among other things, allowed for the bulk collection of Americans' phone data (see Sherfinski 2015). Moreover, Trump has expressed a general commitment to increased securitization. In an interview with Yahoo! News, for example, Trump warned, "We're going to have to do things that we never did before. . . . And certain things will be done that we never thought would happen in this country in terms of information and learning about the enemy. And so we're going to have to do certain things that were frankly unthinkable a year ago" (quoted in Walker 2015). Ironically, Trump and his associates are also experiencing the glare of the surveillant state in the form of intelligence suggesting some form of collaboration with Russia during the presidential election campaign. With respect to open government data, Trump has not explicitly denounced it, but given that, on the campaign trail, he promised to rescind "every single Obama executive order" (quoted in Kopan 2016), the existence of the executive order of 2013 making open and machine readable the new default for government information is precarious.

The uncertain future of both Data.gov and the principle of openness that informs it leads to the possibility that a neoliberal data-driven transparency that contributes to shareveillant subjectivity is better than no transparency at all. In response to this, I would argue that Trump's style of politics means that calling for more (of the same) transparency in the form of open data might miss the point. The case of Trump's nondisclosure of tax returns illustrates this. According to a poll conducted by Quinnipiac University in August 2016, 62 percent of Republicans wanted to see Trump release his tax returns during the presidential race.[1] However, his continued nondisclosure did not turn out to be a deal breaker for that demographic. Routine transparency measures would have necessitated the publication of Trump's taxes; but even if such a provision had been in place, Trump's claim during the first presidential debate in September 2016 that not paying federal income tax "just made [him] smart" seemed to chime with a prevailing anticommunitarian, antistate, and survival-of-the-fittest spirit. Perhaps this pertains to Judith Butler's comment that Trump "lives above the law, and that is where many of his supporters also want to live" (quoted in Salmon 2016). It certainly does not feel as though open data-driven transparency will be up to the job of keeping a Trump administration in check, because Trump seems unconcerned

1. See https://poll.qu.edu/national/release-detail?ReleaseID=2375.

if his worst excesses are revealed. Often, he is the source of those "revelations."

All kinds of misdemeanors and malfeasance came to light during Trump's campaign (sexism, racism, "ableism"), hardly any of which affected his popularity among core supporters. In response to new evidence of bad behavior, Trump was praised for "straight talking" beyond establishment political correctness, for "telling it like it is," even if that meant using "post-truth" tactics that require neither logic nor evidence. His candid and undiplomatic tweets are exemplary in this regard. It is easy to cast this populist rhetorical strategy as itself an obfuscating performance of openness. The relationship here between concealment and revelation is complex. As Geoffrey Bennington (2011, 26) comments, "uncovering secrets always might unveil the fact that the truth this revealed is part of a greater system of secrecy, and merely a supplementary fold in the structure of veiling itself. Enlightenment always might in fact be the dupe of apparent transparency, and transparency might still be a kind of veil." Such logic pertains as much to shareveillant transparency as it does to Trump's "frank" mode of commentary.

What of the data that has already been shared with its public? In early 2017, transparency advocates, political historians, archivists, and environmental activists were busy backing up federal data sets and Web pages for fear that a Trump administration will take down what is available (Gerstein 2016). For example, the End of Term Web Archive[2] called for assistance with its "End of Term Presidential Harvest."[3] This was a collaboration between a group of university, nonprofit, and gov-

2. http://eotarchive.cdlib.org/index.html.
3. http://digital2.library.unt.edu/nomination/eth2016/about/.

ernment libraries. It called on technologically competent researchers to identify federal Web pages in need of preservation for the record. Because of the technological restrictions sometimes placed on downloading data even while that data can be searched in multiple ways online, data sets present a particular problem for archivists; much open data is therefore still vulnerable, despite Web archiving.

Concern about loss of data (a move not from "open" to "closed" in the terms that I have been discussing, but "open" to "erased") extends beyond the library community. This has prompted Abbie Grotke of the Library of Congress to comment, "This year, we've seen a lot of these activities just sprout up. We are losing control a little bit" (quoted in Gerstein 2016). She could be referring to events such as the University of Toronto's "Guerrilla Archiving Event: Saving Environmental Data from Trump" on December 17, 2016: an organized hackathon intended to assist the efforts of the End of Term Web Archive to preserve information and data from the Environmental Protection Agency, especially data relating to climate change and water, air, and toxics programs.[4] Grotke might, however, also be thinking of lone operators like Maxwell Ogden, a programmer for the open data sharing project Dat Project, who decided to archive all nine gigabits of the data on the Obama administration's open.whitehouse.gov pages on Inauguration Day (see Lynch 2017), or Russ Kick, who established the Memory Hole, which archives deleted Web pages and social media feeds relating to Trump.[5] Kick's endeavor is obviously concerned with preserving a different form of content to that contained by data sets but is nevertheless prompted by concerns regarding ac-

4. See https://ischool.utoronto.ca/content/guerrilla-archiving -event-saving-environmental-data-trump.

5. See http://thememoryhole2.org/blog/trump-deletions.

countability and the public record that also shape a desire to preserve statistical data.

Once Trump came into office, any indication that data was going missing or being displaced was met with concern. For example, *Meritalk,* a public–private news outlet focused on government information technology, ran an article reflecting the unease in transparency quarters that data on open.whitehouse. gov had been badly archived in formats that meant data was compromised in terms of usability (Lynch 2017). In fact, deleting federal records is against the law, and because of the multiple copies made of key data such as that recorded by NASA's Lunar Reconnaissance Orbiter, it is almost impossible for some data sets to disappear. Consequently, science journalist Megan Molteni (2017) comments that citizens should be less worried about archiving existing data and more concerned about making sure that data sets are renewed, something that the Trump administration has not committed to: "Archiving is inherently static. . . . Datasets, on the other hand, are dynamic. And keeping open data pipelines, and the funding that makes them possible, is what scientists and concerned citizens should really be worried about." A commitment to feeding data sets with new content is in the balance. Although the Senate passed the Open Government Data Act at the end of the 114th congress, the act has yet to pass in Congress. Though traditionally a bipartisan issue, open government data may well feel overly associated with the Obama administration to pass during Trump's presidency.

Despite clear limitations, guerilla archiving practices could still constitute examples of "commoning." Of preserving data and information for future, unanticipated, and as yet unknown forms of sharing, which transcend the sometimes shareveillant origin and context of the data concerned? This uncontrolled dissemination and use of open data that operates without ref-

erence to the data economy is one response to the present political climate in the United States. I suspect a tactical opacity will
also be an important tool when closed data practices like dataveillance are put in the service of "post-truth" discursive formations that trade in fear to demarcate insiders and outsiders
on the basis of apparently legible, "transparent," and knowable
identities like "the Muslim" or "the illegal immigrant." Sharing
and veillance may well have a different relationship in this new
distribution, and we will have to intervene accordingly.

Acknowledgments

I would like to thank Joanna Zylinska, Gary Hall, Zach Blas, Vian Bakir, and Stephen Armstrong for their intellectual input at various stages of this project. I am also grateful for the support I have received from my colleagues at King's College London and the assistance from the team at University of Minnesota Press. Last, I would like to thank the MA students at King's College London who have taken my Cultures of Secrecy module over the past few years, helping me to think through and with the politics of the secret.

Bibliography

Adema, Janneke, and Gary Hall. 2013. "The Political Nature of the Book: Artists' Books and Radical Open Access." *New Formations* 78: 138–56.

Ahmed, Sara. 2010. Foreword to *Secrecy and Silence in the Research Process: Feminist Reflections,* edited by Róisí Ryan-Flood and Rosalind Gill, xvi–xxi. London: Routledge.

Althusser, Louis. 1971. "Ideology and Ideological State Apparatuses." In *Lenin and Philosophy, and Other Essays,* translated by B. Brewster, 127–88. London: New Left Books.

Andrejevic, Mark, and Kelly Gates. 2014. "Big Data Surveillance: Introduction." *Surveillance and Society* 12, no. 2: 185–96. http://library.queensu.ca/ojs/index.php/surveillance-and-society/issue/view/Big%20Data.

Bataille, Georges. 1991. *The Accursed Share.* New York: Zone Books.

——, ed. 1997. *Encyclopedia Acephalica.* London: Atlas Arkhive.

Belk, Russell. 2010. "Sharing." *Journal of Consumer Research* 36, no. 5: 715–34.

Benkler, Yochai. 2006. *The Wealth of Networks.* New Haven, Conn.: Yale University Press.

Bennington, Geoffrey. 2011. "Kant's Open Secret." *Theory, Culture, and Society* 28, no. 7–8: 26–40.

Birchall, Clare. 2015. "'Data.gov-in-a-Box': Delimiting Transparency." *European Journal of Social Theory* 18, no. 2: 185–202.

Bollier, David, and Silke Helfrich. 2012. "Introduction: The Commons as a Transformative Vision." In *The Wealth of the Commons: A World beyond Market and State,* edited by David Bollier and Silke Helfrich. http://wealthofthecommons.org/essay/introduction-commons-transformative-vision.

Broad, Ellen. 2015. "Closed, Shared, Open Data: What's in a Name?" *Open Data Institute* (blog), September 17. https://theodi.org/blog /closed-shared-open-data-whats-in-a-name.

Brown, Wendy. 2005. *Edgework: Critical Essays on Knowledge and Politics.* Princeton, N.J.: Princeton University Press.

Brunton, Finn, and Helen Nissenbaum. 2015. *Obfuscation: A User's Guide for Privacy and Protest.* Cambridge, Mass.: MIT Press.

Bulajewski, Mike. 2014. "The Cult of Sharing." *Metareader* (blog), August 5. http://www.metareader.org/post/the-cult-of-sharing .html.

Campbell-Moore, Owen. 2013. "Hide Secret Messages in Facebook Photos Using This New Chrome Extension." *Owen Campbell-Moore* (blog), April 7. http://www.owencampbellmoore.com/blog/2013/04 /hide-secret-messages-in-facebook-photos-using-this-new-chrome -extension/.

Chambers, Samuel A. 2012. *The Lessons of Rancière.* Oxford: Oxford University Press.

Cirio, Paolo. n.d. "About the Participation of the Public." https:// obscurity.online/?/l/About/#Participatory.

Clough, Patricia, Karen Gregory, Benjamin Haber, and R. Joshua Scannel. 2014. "The Datalogical Turn." In *Non-representational Methodologies: Re-envisaging Research,* edited by Phillip Vannini, 146–64. London: Routledge.

Dean, Jodi. 2009. *Democracy and Other Neoliberal Fantasies: Communicative Capitalism and Left Politics.* Durham, N.C.: Duke University Press.

De Angelis, Massimo. 2007. *The Beginning of History: Value Struggles and Global Capital.* London: Pluto.

Deleuze, Gilles. 1992. "Postscript on the Societies of Control." *October* 59: 3–7.

Derrida, Jacques. 1992. *The Gift of Death.* Translated by David Wills. Chicago: University of Chicago Press.

———. 1996. "Remarks on Deconstruction and Pragmatism." In *Deconstruction and Pragmatism,* edited by Chantalle Mouffe, 79– 90. London: Routledge.

Derrida, Jacques, and Maurizio Ferraris. 2001. *A Taste for the Secret.* Cambridge: Polity.

Duffy, Nick. 2016. "19 Pink News Stories People Want the Internet to Forget." *Pink News,* February 2. http://www.pinknews.co.uk/2016 /02/02/bbc-stars-to-crystal-meth-in-anus-19-pinknews-stories -people-want-the-internet-to-forget/.

Eggers, Dave. 2013. *The Circle*. London: Hamish Hamilton.

Elmer, Greg. 2003. *Profiling Machines: Mapping the Personal Information Economy*. Cambridge, Mass.: MIT Press.

Fisher, Mark. 2009. *Capitalist Realism: Is There No Alternative?* Winchester, U.K.: Zero Books.

Federici, Silvia. 2012. "Feminism and the Politics of the Commons." In *The Wealth of the Commons: A World beyond Market and State*, edited by David Bollier and Silke Helfrich. http://wealthofthecommons.org/essay/feminism-and-politics-commons.

Galloway, Alexander. 2004. *Protocol: How Control Exists after Decentralization*. Cambridge, Mass.: MIT Press.

Galloway, Alexander, and Eugene Thacker. 2007. *The Exploit: A Theory of Networks*. Minneapolis: University of Minnesota Press.

Gerstein, Josh. 2016. "Fears Rise of Trump-Era 'Memory Hole' in Federal Data." *Politico,* December 13. http://www.politico.com/story/2016/12/trump-federal-data-fears-232591.

Gilbert, Jeremy. 2008. *Anticapitalism and Culture: Radical Theory and Popular Politics*. Oxford: Berg.

Glissant, Édouard. 1997. *Poetics of Relation*. Translated by Betsy Wing. Ann Arbor: Michigan University Press.

Glissant, Édouard, in conversation with Manthia Diawara. 2011. "One World in Relation." *NKA: Journal of Contemporary African Art* 28: 4–19.

Goldstein, Brett, and Lauren Dyson, eds. 2013. *Beyond Transparency: Open Data and the Future of Civic Innovation*. San Francisco, Calif.: Code for America Press.

Hall, Gary. 2008. *Digitize This Book!* Minneapolis: University of Minnesota Press.

———. 2016. *The Uberfication of the University*. Minneapolis: University of Minnesota Press.

Han, Byung-Chul. 2015. *The Transparency Society*. Stanford, Calif.: Stanford University Press.

Hardt, Michael, and Antonio Negri. 2000. *Empire*. Cambridge, Mass.: Harvard University Press.

———. 2004. *Multitude: War and Democracy in the Age of Empire*. New York: Penguin.

Horkheimer, Max. 1989. "Notes on Institute Activities." In *Critical Theory and Society: A Reader,* edited by Stephen E. Bronner and Douglas Kellner, 264–66. New York: Routledge.

Ingram, Matthew. 2013. "Even the CIA Is Struggling to Deal with the Volume of Real-Time Social Data." *Gigaom,* March 20. https://

gigaom.com/2013/03/20/even-the-cia-is-struggling-to-deal-with
-the-volume-of-real-time-social-data/.

Isin, Engin, and Evelyn Ruppert. 2015. *Being Digital Citizens*. London:
Rowman and Littlefield.

John, Nicholas A. 2013. "Sharing and Web 2.0: The Emergence of a
Keyword." *New Media and Society* 15, no. 2: 167–82.

———. 2014. "Sharing [draft] [#digitalkeywords]." *Culture Digitally*
(blog), May 27. http://culturedigitally.org/2014/05/sharing-draft
-digitalkeywords/.

Johnson, M. Eric, Dan McGuire, and Nicholas D. Willey. 2008. "The
Evolution of the Peer-to-Peer File Sharing Industry and the
Security Risks for Users." Paper presented at the forty-first Hawaii
International Conference on System Sciences, Waikoloa, Hawaii,
January 8–10. https://www.computer.org/csdl/proceedings/hicss
/2008/3075/00/30750383.pdf.

Kember, Sarah, and Joanna Zylinska. 2012. *Life after New Media:
Mediation as Vital Process*. Cambridge, Mass.: MIT Press.

Kitchin, Rob. 2014. *The Data Revolution: Big Data, Open Data, Data
Infrastructures, and Their Consequences*. London: Sage.

Kopan, Tal. 2016. "Could a President Trump Reverse Obama's
Regulations on 'Day One'?" CNN Politics, September 28. http://
edition.cnn.com/2016/09/28/politics/trump-executive-action
-obama/.

Kosofsky Sedgwick, Eve. 2003. "Paranoid Reading and Reparative
Reading, or You're So Paranoid, You Probably Think This Essay Is
about You." In *Touching Feeling: Affect, Pedagogy, Performativity*,
123–51. Durham, N.C.: Duke University Press.

Lessig, Lawrence. 2009. "Against Transparency." *New Republic*,
October 9. https://newrepublic.com/article/70097/against
-transparency.

Lovink, Geert. 2016. *Social Media Abyss: Critical Internet Cultures and
the Force of Negation*. Cambridge: Polity.

Lütticken, Sven. 2006. *Secret Publicity: Essays on Contemporary Art*.
Rotterdam, Netherlands: NAi.

Lynch, Morgan. 2017. "White House Open Data Disappears, Raising
Transparency Questions." *Merital*, February 16. https://www
.meritalk.com/articles/white-house-open-data-disappears
-transparency-donald-trump-sunlight-foundation/.

MacKinnon, Catherine. 1989. *Toward a Feminist Theory of the State*.
Cambridge, Mass.: Harvard University Press.

Mann, Steve. 2013. "Veillance and Reciprocal Transparency:

Surveillance versus Sousveillance, AR Glass, Lifeglogging, and Wearable Computing." http://wearcam.org/veillance/veillance.pdf.

Maude, Francis. 2012. "Open Data White Paper: Unleashing the Potential." https://data.gov.uk/sites/default/files/Open_data_White_Paper.pdf.

McDermott, John. 2015. "WTF Is Data Leakage?" *Digiday* (blog), January 27. http://digiday.com/platforms/what-is-data-leakage/.

McKinsey Global Institute. 2013. "Unlocking Innovation and Performance with Liquid Information." November. http://www.mckinsey.com/business-functions/business-technology/our-insights/open-data-unlocking-innovation-and-performance-with-liquid-information.

McStay, Andy. 2014. *Privacy and Philosophy: New Media and Affective Protocol.* Bern, Switzerland: Peter Lang.

Melley, Tim. 2012. *The Covert Sphere: Secrecy, Fiction, and the National Security State.* Ithaca, N.Y.: Cornell University Press.

Molteni, Megan. 2017. "Old-Guard Archivists Keep Federal Data Safer Than You Think." *Wired,* February 19. https://www.wired.com/2017/02/army-old-guard-archivers-federal-data-safer-think/.

Morozov, Evgeny. 2013. *To Save Everything, Click Here: The Folly of Technological Solutionism.* London: Allen Lane.

Open Data Institute. 2015. "The Economic Impact of Open Data: What Do We Already Know?" November 2. https://medium.com/@ODIHQ/the-economic-impact-of-open-data-what-do-we-already-know-1a119c1958a0#.t3b53aa8j.

Peters, Benjamin, ed. 2016. *Digital Keywords: A Vocabulary of Information Society and Culture.* Princeton, N.J.: Princeton University Press.

Prainsack, Barbara. 2015. "Why We Should Stop Talking about Data Sharing." *DNA Digest* (blog), December 1. http://dnadigest.org/why-we-should-stop-talking-about-data-sharing/.

Rancière, Jacques. 1992. "Politics, Identification, and Subjectivization." *October* 61 (Summer): 58–64.

———. 2004a. *The Philosopher and His Poor.* Translated by John Drury, Corinne Oster, and Andrew Parker. Edited by Andrew Parker. Durham, N.C.: Duke University Press.

———. 2004b. *The Politics of Aesthetics: Distribution of the Sensible.* Translated by Gabriel Rockhill. London: Continuum.

Reuters. 2013. "Protesters March in Washington against NSA Spying." October 26. http://www.reuters.com/article/us-usa-security-protest-idUSBRE99P0B420131027.

Salmon, Christian. 2016. "Trump, Fascism, and the Construction of 'the People': An Interview with Judith Butler." *Verso* (blog), December 29. http://www.versobooks.com/blogs/3025-trump -fascism-and-the-construction-of-the-people-an-interview-with -judith-butler.

Sherfinksi, David. 2015. "Donald Trump on NSA Phone-Snooping Program: 'I Err on the Side of Security.'" *Washington Times,* December 2. http://www.washingtontimes.com/news/2015/dec/2 /donald-trump-nsa-phone-snooping-program-i-err-side/.

Shirky, Clay. 2008. *Here Comes Everybody: The Power of Organizing without Organizations.* London: Penguin.

Shore, Cris. 2008. "Audit Culture and Illiberal Governance: Universities and the Politics of Accountability." *Anthropological Theory* 8, no. 3: 278–98.

Smith, Aaron Lake. 2010. "Vive le Tarnac Nine! The French Tradition of Brainy Sabotage Lives On." *Vice,* April 3. http://www.vice.com /read/vive-le-tarnac-nine-407-v17n4.

Spivack, Nova. 2013. "The Post-privacy World." *Wired,* July. http:// www.wired.com/insights/2013/07/the-post-privacy-world/.

Tiqqun. (2001) 2009. *The Cybernetic Hypothesis.* Translated by Anon. http://cybernet.jottit.com/.

Turner, Fred. 2006. *From Counterculture to Cyberculture: Stewart Brand, the Whole Earth Network, and the Rise of Digital Utopianism.* Chicago: University of Chicago Press.

Walker, Hunter. 2015. "Donald Trump Has Big Plans for 'Radical Islamic' Terrorists, 2016 and 'That Communist' Bernie Sanders." Yahoo! News, November 19. https://www.yahoo.com/news/donald -trump-has-big-plans-1303117537878070.html.

White House. 2013. "Executive Order—Making Open and Machine Readable the New Default for Government Information." May 9. https://www.whitehouse.gov/the-press-office/2013/05/09 /executive-order-making-open-and-machine-readable-new-default -government-.

Williams, Raymond. 1976. *Keywords: A Vocabulary of Culture and Society.* London: Fontana.

Wittel, Andreas. 2011. "Qualities of Sharing and Their Transformations in the Digital Age." *International Review of Information Ethics* 15: 3–8.

World Bank. 2014. *Open Data for Economic Growth.* https:// openknowledge.worldbank.org/handle/10986/19997.

Clare Birchall is senior lecturer at King's College London. She is author of *Knowledge Goes Pop: From Conspiracy Theory to Gossip* and coeditor of *New Cultural Studies: Adventures in Theory*.